GERIATRIC CAT
HEALTH & CARE
JOURNAL

A Complete Toolkit for the
GERIATRIC CAT CAREGIVER

DR. MARY GARDNER

ISBN: 978-1-956343-07-6

Ed: 1

Researcher and editor: Dr. Theresa Entriken

Interior design by: Ljiljana Pavkov
Illustrations by: Dusan Pavlic
Book cover design by: Victoria Black

Disclaimer

This book is not intended as a medical textbook. Every pet should receive an examination by their veterinarian prior to starting any treatment. Seek your veterinarian's advice if you have any concerns with your pet.

If you happen to have a dog, I have created a journal for them too! Check out all my books at greymuzzlvet.com/books

Publisher: Rolled Toe Publishing (Books@GreyMuzzleVet.com)

   /drmarygardner  greymuzzlevet

Introduction

You adore your cat. You provide their loving care, and assure the certainty and comfort of home. In return, your cat offers companionship that makes your life sweeter. This good life can seem everlasting! Then seemingly all too soon, your cat may begin to show subtle signs of the burdens that Father Time can bring.

Perhaps playtimes spark less joy for your cat and chase games end sooner. Their favorite perch on high sits unoccupied because they prefer a new spot that requires less of a leap to get to. They spend less time curiously peering through the screen of an open window, and more moments seeking the warmth of your lap. Your cat may leave meals unfinished, or begin to look thinner and scruffier for no apparent reason. Their meows soften, except perhaps in the middle of the night when they wander through rooms and yowl alarmingly loudly. Your cat may stop reliably using the litter box. As cats traverse their senior years, subtle age-related developments take hold. And without your careful attention, drastic changes may seem to occur overnight.

As a devoted pet parent, you know your cat's attitude, activities, and behavior best. It's helpful to track these characteristics in a pet health journal such as this one, or on a calendar, or in your phone, or using an app—whichever method works best for you. When you note changes or when symptoms arise, mention them and any concerns you have to your veterinary team—throughout your cat's life, of course, and especially during your cat's elder years. Some changes or symptoms (such as drinking more water, vomiting frequently, sleeping in unusual spots) may signal serious health issues, and other changes (such as more curiosity, less restlessness, better appetite) may signify health improvements.

Keeping a pet health journal also helps you identify factors that may have contributed to the symptoms or improvements you note. Jotting down events—such as when you switch your cat's diet, have overnight houseguests, start or stop giving a medication to your cat, board your cat, place steps to help your cat access a preferred perch, or have your veterinarian clean your cat's teeth—can provide clues that point to a cause of an illness or a resolution of an ailment. These clues can also help you illustrate trends, map recurring problems, and head off a serious health condition in your cat.

This journal is a companion to my upcoming book "Nine Lives Are Not Enough – A Practical Guide to Caring for your Geriatric Cat." Together these resources provide a wealth of information and support as you care for your aging feline friend. The journal pages, questionnaires, logs, lists, assessments, and other templates provided will help you document and keep important information handy and organized. Use them all, or select those most relevant to you and your cat. This journal can also make partnering with your veterinarian easier as you continue to provide your kitty's best care! If you need more of these pages, you can find many of them on a special webpage I built. Use this QR code to access them:

Cat Journal
Templates

I hope the tools contained in this journal allow you to better assess and manage your geriatric cat's health, feel empowered to make the best decisions, and continue enjoying your time with your beloved feline family member.

 Dr. Mary examining her own cat Lilu who had diabetes and kidney disease.

Table of Contents

GERIATRIC CAT
HEALTH & CARE
JOURNAL

1

My cat's care team

Start by jotting down your cat's key details along with a handy list of all those who help care for your kitty.

My cat's name:
....

Date of birth: .... Adoption date: ....

Breed: .... Sex: .... Spayed or Neutered (Yes/No) ....

Veterinary Clinic Name and Address:
....

Veterinary Clinic Phone Number:
....

Primary Care Veterinarian:
....

Emergency Veterinary Hospital Name, Address, Phone:
....
....

Boarding Facility Information:
....

Kitty Daycare Information:
....

Cat Sitter Information:
....

Pet Insurance Information:
....

Microchip Information:
....

Emergency Caretaker Contact Information:
....

Other Important Contacts:
....
....

2

Health journal

Have you ever visited your doctor for an annual examination but then afterward mentally kicked yourself because you forgot to ask about a potential new health concern you noticed over the last couple months? Or maybe your doctor asked whether you'd been experiencing something that you hadn't considered a problem, but that turned out to be an early sign of a bigger issue? Similar situations often happen when pet parents visit their veterinarian. During veterinary visits or in times of illness, it can be hard for you to remember the nuances about changes you've noticed in your cat. So it's helpful to keep a health journal for your senior or geriatric cat. A journal will help you think about and recognize changes in your cat that may otherwise go unnoticed. Use the blank journal pages provided here, or create your own.

Write your observations about the types of normal and abnormal behaviors, changes, and symptoms your cat shows. Your entries may include all the details or serve as quick, general notes that support your recall abilities. To help, I've created a list of "Geriatric Cat Health Observations" questions for you to noodle on as you begin to journal about your cat's health. If your responses indicate changes in your cat, bring them up with your veterinarian. Review the question list every four to six months, to help you keep closer tabs on whether changes signal worsening trends that might otherwise catch you unaware.

In addition, take photos and videos of your cat at six-month intervals, and date each one to help you and your veterinarian monitor changes in your cat's appearance and behavior. Beyond the health observations questions and blank journal pages, I've provided supplemental tools to help while you care for your geriatric cat, including forms to track your cat's specific symptoms, diagnostic tests and findings, diagnoses, treatments, schedule changes, and more.

Geriatric Cat Health Observations

Eating/drinking

- What are your cat's favorite foods and treats? *(Record on the Nutrition and Treat Log on page 19)*

  ....

- Have your cat's food preferences changed in the last year?

  ....

- Has your cat's appetite decreased or increased?

  ....

- Are special enticements or is other assistance needed to get your cat to eat?

  ....

- Does your cat drop food while eating or have trouble chewing or swallowing?

  ....

- Does your cat have an increased thirst?

  ....

- Does your cat vomit hairballs, food, or liquid? How often?

  ....

Weight

- What is your cat's current weight?

  ....

- Has your cat lost weight without being on a diet or without getting extra exercise?

  ....

- When you pet your cat, can you more easily feel your cat's spine, hips, or ribs?

  ....

- Has your cat been gaining weight? Does your cat appear to have more belly fat?

  ....

Sleep

- Where does your cat prefer to sleep?

....

- How many hours does your cat sleep during an average day?

....

- Does your cat sleep peacefully?

....

- What does your cat do if they get up during the night?

....

- Does your cat sleep more during the day than they used to and less at night?

....

- Does your cat sleep more overall?

....

- Has your cat started sleeping in unusual or out-of-the way locations?

....

Activity level

- What are your cat's favorite activities, toys, and games?

....

- Who are your cat's favorite people?

....

- Who are your cat's least favorite beings (new visitors, neighborhood cats, neighborhood dogs, anything in the backyard, etc)

....

- Does your cat have other favorite animal friends or playmates?

....

- Has your cat started resting in out-of-the-way places (closet, guest bedroom, in a corner, under the bed)?

....

- Has your cat's activity decreased?

....

- If so, over what time period – the last few days, weeks, or months – or during the last year?

....

Strength and vitality

- Has your cat's energy decreased in the last year?

....

- Does your cat seem less interested in playing or exploring new things?

....

- Is your cat weaker during exercise or less tolerant of exercise?

....

Mobility

- Does your cat "bunny hop" down the stairs? (This may indicate joint pain.)

....

- Does your cat less frequently jump on or off the bed, couch, or other favorite perch?

....

- Have your cat's scratching post preferences changed?

....

- Does your cat "sharpen" their claws less often?

....

- Does your cat drag their toes?

....

- Has your cat's gait changed (walks slower or limps)?

....

Urine, feces, and litter box use

• Have you noticed an increase or decrease in urination?

....

• Any urination or fecal accidents outside of the litter box?

....

• Has the appearance or consistency of your cat's feces changed? Any diarrhea? Constipation?

....

• Does your cat pass a fecal ball without seeming to notice?

....

• Does your cat involuntarily leak urine?

....

• Does your cat lick their hind end excessively?

....

Ears, eyes, nose, mouth, throat, and breathing

• Have you noticed a change in your cat's hearing?

....

• Is your cat more or less reactive to noises?

....

• Does your cat have vision problems in bright light? In dim light? At night?

....

• Does your cat have a runny nose or sneeze often?

....

• Does your cat have watery or gooey discharge around the eyes?

....

• Does your cat have bad breath?

....

• Does your cat's meow sound different?

....

• Does your cat breathe faster or heavier?

....

• Any coughing?

....

• Does your cat purr more often than usual? Or less often?

....

Skin, coat, and toenails

• Does your cat have increased or excessive itching?

....

• Have you found lumps or bumps on or under the skin?

....

• Does your cat have unpleasant or odd skin or ear odor?

....

• Does your cat excessively lick or chew their skin or fur?

....

• Is your cat's skin or fur flaky, dry, or oily?

....

• Does your cat's fur look unkempt?

....

• Does your cat groom himself less often? (Does your cat have mats or a soiled rear end?)

....

• Have you noticed longer claws?

....

• Does your cat enjoy being brushed or combed?

....

- Is your cat's coat thinning? Dull?

- Does your cat shed excessively or have areas of hair loss?

Temperature and overall comfort

- Does your cat seek out new or unusual areas to rest that are warm, cold, soft, sunny, or hard?

- Does your cat's fur seem fluffed up?

- Does your cat sit in a hunched position?

- Does she shiver or tremble?

- Does your cat pant, or breathe with an open mouth?

Mentation
(If your cat exhibits these signs, see also the "Cognitive Assessment and Health Concerns for Cats" form on pages 21-24.)

- Is your cat less interested in greeting you when you get home?

- Has your cat been less interactive with the family?

- Is your cat more clingy or anxious?

- Does your cat pace during the day or night?

• Does your cat stare off into space?

....

• Does your cat seem irritable or act more aggressively?

....

• Does your cat seem disoriented or distant?

....

• Does your cat become agitated at certain times of the day?

....

• Does your cat get stuck in odd locations or appear lost?

....

• Does your cat vocalize inappropriately (meow at night for no apparent reason)?

....

• Does your cat circle? (If so, is it one direction or both?)

....

• Has your cat had a seizure?

....

NOTES

....

....

....

....

....

....

....

3

Meals and treats

Nutrition is an integral component of your cat's wellness, and diet is a key factor in helping prevent or manage many different ailments. So an important component of your cat's veterinary visits includes discussing your cat's diet, appetite, caloric intake, and activity levels. As part of your pet's nutritional assessment, your veterinarian may ask you to provide a diet history for your cat.

An accurate diet history can be difficult to recall during the veterinary visit, so use the form I've created here and update it as needed, for example if you need to switch to a different diet or if you add a new treat. Or at the very least, take a picture of your pet's food and treats in their original packaging so the information is easily readable for you to share with your veterinarian.

Nutrition and Treat Log:

Daily diet (brand and name, type [kibble, canned, fresh, frozen], flavor, or home-cooked diet recipe [with all ingredients and amounts]):

Amount fed per meal (cups or ounces):

Mealtime frequency:

Daily treats (brand and name, type, flavor):

Table foods my cat receives, amounts, and frequency fed:

Date new diet was introduced (brand/name, type, flavor, amount, and frequency fed):

Date new treats were introduced ((brand/name, type, flavor, amounts, frequency fed):

Date new table foods were introduced (types, amounts, frequency fed):

Foods or treats used to deliver medications:

Dietary supplements (record here or on the medication log in Section 8):

Dental chews or treats:

Water additives or broths (brand or types and amounts):

4

Cognitive health assessment

Changes in a cat's typical behavior or temperament at any age can signal illness or a new behavior problem. But some geriatric cats exhibit odd behaviors and signs of mental deficits that can't otherwise be attributed to illness, behavioral problems, or typical age-related decline in eyesight or hearing. Instead, their out-of-character conduct may be caused by changes in their brain that are similar to the symptoms and brain changes that people with Alzheimer's disease and senile dementia have. In cats, these signs of age-related mental decline and brain abnormalities are called *cognitive dysfunction syndrome*. This disorder tends to progress with age, and it can seriously affect a cat's and their family's daily quality of life.

A cat's behavior changes may be subtle at first, and pet parents tend to attribute them to their cats "just getting old" or "having senior moments." They can be as subtle as getting a little confused and turned around in the house, or as severe as anxious wandering and yowling in the middle of the night. Although there is no cure for cognitive dysfunction in cats, the sooner we catch it, the better chance we may have to slow its progression. Recognizing the signs of cognitive dysfunction earlier in the course of the disease gives cats and pet parents a better chance to effectively manage their cats' signs and relish more happy, good-quality-of-life days together. Apparently healthy cats can show signs of cognitive impairment as early as 7 years of age! Cognitive deficits tend to progress, but the rate of these changes varies—they may progress slowly or quickly.

Use the "Cognitive Assessment and Health Concerns for Cats" checklist to monitor your cat, and go over it with your veterinarian if you notice changes. A diagnostic test isn't yet available to pinpoint cognitive dysfunction, so veterinarians must make a *diagnosis of exclusion*. This means we look first for another medical condition or behavioral problem that could be causing the pet's signs. Your veterinarian may ask you to complete a questionnaire or checklist designed to screen senior cats for signs of cognitive dysfunction (similar to the checklist I provide here).

Complete this checklist and share it with your veterinarian during your cat's semi-annual examinations. Schedule a veterinary visit sooner anytime your cat's signs concern you, or if your cat exhibits any of these signs once a week or more.

Cat Cognitive
Assessment
Template

Cognitive Assessment and Health Concerns for Cats

Date .... Pet's Name .... Age ....

Category	Sign	Does not occur or is not applicable	Occurs once a month	Occurs once a week	Occurs once a day/ night	Occurs more than once a day/night
VOCALIZATION	Vocalizes more than usual during the day or evening (meows or yowls)					
	Vocalizes more than normal during nighttime sleeping hours (meows or yowls)					
INTERACTIONS	More clingy/seeks more attention/more interest in being petted					
	Hiding/sleeping in unusual places					
	Less interest in being petted					
	Irritable or aggressive with family members					
	Irritable or aggressive with housemate pets					
	Less interest in greeting family members					
	More aloof/seeks less attention					
SLEEP/WAKE CYCLE	Asleep more than usual during the day					
	Awake more than usual during the night					
	Paces/wanders at night					
HOUSE SOILING	Urinates inappropriately in the house/outside the litter box					
	Defecates inappropriately in the house/outside the litter box					
	Urinates but seems unaware					
	Defecates but seems unaware					

Category	Sign	Does not occur or is not applicable	Occurs once a month	Occurs once a week	Occurs once a day/ night	Occurs more than once a day/night
DISORIENTATION	Appears lost/wanders between rooms without purpose					
	Paces back and forth excessively or circles					
	Stares into space or stares absently at the floor or walls					
	Stands in corners					
	Gets stuck under or behind objects					
	Doesn't seem to recognize family members or housemate pets					
	Doesn't seem to recognize or is startled by familiar objects					
	Walks or bumps into doors or walls					
	Has trouble finding treats dropped on the floor					
	Less interested in or less reactive to sights and sounds					
	Has trouble finding food or water bowl					
ANXIETY	Increased anxiety when owners are away/doesn't like being left alone					
	Increased fear of new places/locations					
	More reactive to sights and sounds					
	Agitated or restless during the day or evening					
	Agitated or restless during nighttime sleep hours					

Category	Sign	Does not occur or is not applicable	Occurs once a month	Occurs once a week	Occurs once a day/ night	Occurs more than once a day/night
ACTIVITY	Less or no interest in play or toys					
	Less or no interest in play with housemate pets					
	Less or no interest in self-grooming					
	Less or no interest in exploring					
	Exhibits repetitive behaviors (excessive grooming, licking inanimate objects)					
LEARNING AND MEMORY	Seems to have forgotten trained commands or routines, verbal cues, or name					
	Difficulty learning new commands or routines					
	Decreased focus/hard to get and retain pet's attention					
ADDITIONAL HEALTH CONCERNS	Vomiting					
	Diarrhea					
	Constipation					
	Straining to urinate					
	Straining to defecate					
	Vision loss					
	Hearing loss					
	Hair loss or thinning					
	Decreased appetite					
	Decreased water consumption					
	Increased appetite					
	Increased water consumption					

Category	Sign	Does not occur or is not applicable	Occurs once a month	Occurs once a week	Occurs once a day/ night	Occurs more than once a day/night
ADDITIONAL HEALTH CONCERNS	Hesitant to jump up or down from favorite spots (couch, bed, table, cat tree)					
	Hesitant or unwilling to use stairs					
	Limping					
	Hesitant or unwilling to use scratching post					
	Weakness or sluggishness					

Resources for Cognitive Assessment Checklist

Černá P, Gardiner H, Sordo L, et al. Potential Causes of Increased Vocalisation in Elderly Cats with Cognitive Dysfunction Syndrome as Assessed by Their Owners. Animals (Basel). 2020;10(6):1092. Published 2020 Jun 24. doi:10.3390/ani10061092

Landsberg GM, Denenberg S, Araujo JA. Cognitive dysfunction in cats: a syndrome we used to dismiss as 'old age'. J Feline Med Surg. 2010 Nov;12(11):837-48. doi: 10.1016/j.jfms.2010.09.004. PMID: 20974401.

Salvin HE, McGreevy PD, Sachdev PS, et al. The canine cognitive dysfunction rating scale (CCDR): a data-driven and ecologically relevant assessment tool. Vet J. 2011 Jun;188(3):331-6. doi: 10.1016/j.tvjl.2010.05.014. Epub 2010 Jun 12. PMID: 20542455.

Sordo L, Gunn-Moore DA. Cognitive Dysfunction in Cats: Update on Neuropathological and Behavioural Changes Plus Clinical Management. Vet Rec. 2021 Jan;188(1):e3. doi: 10.1002/vetr.3. Epub 2021 Jan 12. PMID: 34651755.

Woodruff D. Cognitive Dysfunction and Related Sleep Disturbances. In: Gardner M, McVety D, eds. Treatment and care of the veterinary geriatric patient. Hoboken, NJ: John Wiley & Sons, 2017;57-76.

5

Symptom record

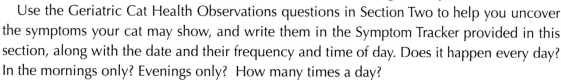

Tracking your cat's symptoms throughout their geriatric years helps you remember and realistically assess whether they have improved, stayed stable, or declined. This can help your veterinarian construct a veterinary care plan for your cat and remodel it as needed along the way.

Use the Geriatric Cat Health Observations questions in Section Two to help you uncover the symptoms your cat may show, and write them in the Symptom Tracker provided in this section, along with the date and their frequency and time of day. Does it happen every day? In the mornings only? Evenings only? How many times a day?

Next, in the Association column, note any circumstance that seems to be connected with the symptom, if applicable. For example, does your cat vomit after you share your ice cream with her? Does your cat meow abnormally at night only after you've returned from a trip? Does he have trouble seeing in the dark? Does she tire easily or cough only when playing with a furry sibling? Did he stop using the litter box when you bought a different brand or type of litter?

Symptom severity is the next aspect to document. Is the symptom mild and your cat doesn't seem too bothered by it, or does it affect her for the rest of the day? You can also note whether it is a mild, moderate, or severe issue for you as the caregiver.

Finally, note improvements—what helps alleviate the symptom? Does your cat use the litter box reliably again after you added one on the main level so she doesn't have to go downstairs to use it? Does your cat sleep through the night after you added a nightlight in the hallway? Does she eat more when you soften or warm her food? Has a new medication helped resolve a specific issue?

Date each entry to help you monitor your cat. You'll notice trends sooner rather than later and can make adjustments faster.

When tracking your geriatric cat's symptoms, keep in mind that with the exception of some conditions that may be treatable and resolve, you're not always seeking perfection or a return to normal. You're looking for ways to help slow the progression of your cat's symptoms and help your cat live well by alleviating as much discomfort as possible—in short, to provide care and love to the best of your abilities. All to help your cat feel better and have a good life quality—and help yourself do so as well.

Cat Symptom Tracker

Symptom tracker

Pet's Name ....

Symptom	Date	Frequency and Time of Day	Association	Severity	Improvements

6

Veterinary visits and procedures

Like elderly people, cats tend to have more health issues and need more medical attention during their last life stage. When cats reach their senior years and beyond, routine veterinary checkups are needed every six months, even for seemingly healthy seniors. Why so many? Veterinary checkups help detect conditions and diseases associated with aging. Looking for and addressing health threats in your furry family members can help them live longer and more comfortably, all while allowing them to stay as active and engaged (and as happy!) as possible. And keep in mind that similar to people who have chronic health problems and need to see their healthcare providers frequently, cats who have chronic medical conditions usually need to see a veterinarian even more often than every six months for rechecks. A cat's final years are the most delicate, and your veterinary team can help shore up the precious time you have left with your cat.

Veterinary Visits and Procedures log

Veterinary Visits and Procedures Log

Visit date .... Veterinary hospital ....

Veterinarian's name ....

Cat's Weight .... Body Condition Score .... Muscle Condition Score ....

Vaccinations .... Claw trim ....

Diagnostic tests done (see also Section 7) ....

....

....

....

Parasite Preventives (Protection from fleas, ticks, heartworms, intestinal parasites), other medications,

supplements, diets, or other treatments prescribed (see also Section 8) ....

....

....

....

....

....

Visit Summary (diagnosis or procedure done, treatment plan) ....

....

....

....

....

....

....

Next visit scheduled for (date): ....

7

Diagnostic tests

I recommend that senior and geriatric cats have routine blood tests (complete blood count, serum chemistry profile [including thyroid hormone measurement]), a urine test (urinalysis), and blood pressure measurement done every six to 12 months. In addition, your cat should have a heartworm test and fecal examination done yearly.

Your cat may have a condition that also requires additional types of blood tests (such as tests for infectious diseases), other diagnostic tests (such as x-rays, ultrasound, electrocardiogram), or frequent rechecks of a specific blood test. Use the Diagnostic Test Tracker to monitor your cat's tests and record a summary of the results.

For pet parents of cats who have diabetes, I've also included a form to monitor glucose and related parameters. And in Section 8, you'll find a form to record insulin injections as well.

Cat Diagnostic
Test Tracker

Cat Glucose
Tracker

Diagnostic Test Tracker

Diagnostic Test Tracker

Pet's Name ....

Date	Test	Result Summary

Glucose Tracker

Pet's Name ....

Date	Blood Glucose Concentration	Urine Glucose	Urine Ketones	Notes (Attitude, Water consumption, Urination, etc)

8

Tracking treatments

It's just as important to keep good notes about your cat's medications, other therapies, and schedule changes as it is to track your cat's symptoms. Such notes are a handy reference for treatments you've tried or changes you've made and their effects.

Log each drug name, dose, frequency (how many times a day it's given) and duration (how long it's to be given), what it's used to treat or manage, and the result (whether it helped or if you noted side effects or new symptoms). If you adjust a dose or the number of times it's given, record that as well (note that all prescription medicine adjustments should be made according to your veterinarian's advice).

Remember to track the medications, supplements, or nutraceuticals that you purchase over-the-counter as well. Also note any other therapy such as surgery, chemotherapy, acupuncture, grooming, massage, and any major schedule change such as boarding.

Remembering whether you gave your cat a medication can be difficult, especially if your cat receives more than one medication, has to take medications more often than twice a day, or if more than one person gives the medication. Multi-dose vitamin/pill containers can make medication times easier to manage.

Here I've provided a general treatment tracker, a medication log to track once or twice a day administration, and a log for therapies given more than twice a day, along with an insulin tracker for pet parents who need to administer insulin.

Treatment Tracker

Cat Medication
Log (2 x)

Cat Medication
Log (multiple)

Cat Insulin
Tracker

Treatment tracker

Pet's Name ....

Date	Medication (and other therapy) or change in schedule	Dose	Frequency and Duration	What it's for	Result

Medication Administration Log (once or twice a day)

Pet's Name ....

Date	Medication	AM	PM

Medication Administration Log (more than twice a day)

Pet's Name ....

Date	Medication	Time 1	Time 2	Time 3	Time 4	Time 5	Time 6

Insulin Tracker

Pet's Name ....

Date	Feeding Time Morning	Insulin Dose and Time / Morning	Feeding Time Evening	Insulin Dose and Time / Evening

9
Counting breaths

If your cat has a respiratory condition or heart disease, then keeping tabs on their breathing rate and effort is especially important. The Respiratory Rate Tracker is perfect for that! While your cat is resting or sleeping, count how often they take a breath in 20 seconds and multiply that by three to determine their respiratory rate per minute. Your cat's ideal resting respiratory rate may depend on what medical condition your cat has and which medications your cat receives, so your veterinarian will advise you on the appropriate breaths per minute range. However, in general, if your cat's breathing rate is consistently over 30 breaths per minute while he is relaxed and resting or sleeping, call your veterinarian to schedule an evaluation.

Cat Respiratory
Rate Tracker

Respiratory Rate Tracker

Respiratory Rate Tracker

Count the number of breaths your cat takes in 20 seconds and multiply it by three to calculate the number of breaths per minute.

Pet's Name ....

My pet's resting respiratory rate/minute should be (according to my vet): ....

Date	Notes about the day/how my pet was breathing	Resting Rate/Minute AM	Resting Rate/Minute PM

10

Goals of care

My good friend and human hospice and palliative medicine physician BJ Miller co-wrote the book *A Beginner's Guide to the End: Practical Advice for Living Life and Facing Death*. It's a valuable reference for anyone facing a friend's, family member's, or their own end of life. I've refined a few tools I've been using over the years in my veterinary hospice practice based on some wonderful concepts from BJ's book. Based on the care goals exercise that BJ Miller outlines in his book, I advise pet parents to create a "Goals of Care" journal entry as well.

Thinking about your goals of care for your cat encourages you to collect your thoughts about the influences on your cat's and your experiences near the end of your cat's life. Writing down these goals helps you realistically assess the circumstances you're facing with regard to your cat's ailments and how much treatment you're willing to pursue. It helps you decide which goals and activities are most important for your cat and you, establish which compromises you're willing to make, and create a road map for how you'll meet your goals of care. This exercise also helps you consider whether your goals for your cat match up with your abilities to reach them.

Here are examples of care-oriented questions to ask yourself that will help you identify priorities as your pet experiences the limitations and illnesses that aging brings.

CIRCUMSTANCES: Write what you know about your cat's diagnosis or condition, and list the resources available to you. Do you need family members and friends to help? Are they available and willing to help? Can you talk with your veterinarian regularly about your cat's care? As your cat's caregiver, what are your financial, physical, emotional, and time limitations?

GOALS: Write what you want to do for your cat and for yourself as his caregiver. Do you want your cat to receive all possible curative treatments? Or would you rather focus solely on

Cat
Goals of Care

relieving symptoms? Would you like to supplement your care with veterinary hospice care? Do you have a bucket list you'd like to fulfill for your cat? Do you want to plan for your cat to die at home rather than at the veterinary hospital? Do you want a veterinarian to end your cat's dying process before active suffering occurs? How would you like to memorialize your cat?

COMPROMISES: Truthfully draw your line in the sand. What trade-offs are you willing to make and not make? Will you delay travel for months because your cat needs extensive care? Will you allow others to care for your cat if you need to be away? Does it work with your schedule and finances to take your cat in for cancer treatments? Are you OK with not trying or not providing certain therapies that may give you more time with your cat? Are you OK with not starting or with stopping certain therapies that are unlikely to help your cat?

ROAD MAP: List your next action items for providing care and meeting your goals within the guardrails of your compromises and limitations. Do you need to put up baby gates to keep your cat out of certain areas of the house, or install night lights? Do you need to investigate veterinary physical rehabilitation therapy options? Would you like to ask your veterinarian to show you how to administer fluids under your cat's skin at home? Would you like to buy a cat stroller to fulfill an outdoor outing bucket list item? Do you need to schedule a veterinary examination to provide comfort care or discuss hospice? Do you wish to explore options for aftercare of your cat's body?

You may need to reexamine your goals of care every month as your cat's condition and your situation change. Your cat's care may be easy one month, but the next month you may feel overwhelmed in trying to control your cat's symptoms. I also suggest discussing your care goals with your veterinarian—this allows your veterinarian to understand your wishes and direct your cat's care appropriately.

GOALS OF CARE

Pet's Name .... Date ....

Circumstances	
Goals	
Compromises	
Road Map	

11 The adventures of a lifetime

I often suggest that pet parents create a bucket list of all the things they want to do for their cat or allow their cat to experience before they say their final goodbye. When you're thinking about the list, consider: What makes your cat your cat? What brings him pure joy? What brings her ordinary happiness? What 10 things do you want him to experience before you say goodbye?

Add to the list or make different plans if your cat's health status changes. Start checking things off while you can both still relish the activities—whether it's weeks, months, or years before your cat earns angel wings.

Bucket list activities needn't be extravagant. I think it's safe to say most cats, especially seniors, savor the comforts of a stable routine and simple surprises. Two of the activities on my cat's bucket list were getting a daily brush in the sun and a fresh catnip toy every week. I love bucket lists because when it comes time to say goodbye to your cat, having checked off those special activities and experiences diminishes regret. It allows you to focus fully on the tender moments you have with your beloved cat in their final hours.

Cat Bucket List

 Tigger's Bucket List which was completed before his family said goodbye.

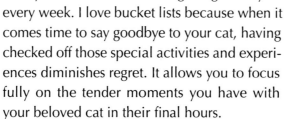

Tigger's Bucket List

- Let him go down in the basement
- Lots of walks in his backpack carrier
- Leash time supervised when the weather is nice
- Cat nip party
- Snacks at least once a day
- Lots of lap time and pets
- Professional photo shoot
- Telling him I ♥ him every day
- One new treat or toy every two weeks

_____'s
BUCKET LIST

PHOTO

- [ ]
- [ ]
- [ ]
- [ ]
- [ ]
- [ ]
- [ ]
- [ ]
- [ ]
- [ ]
- [ ]
- [ ]
- [ ]

12

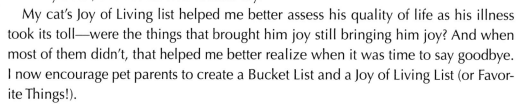

Joyful living

One of my patient's families once wrote a "Joy of Living" list for their dog, and I like that twist, and it works for cats, too. It may overlap with a Bucket List, but it's a bit different. For example, with my own cat, I realized I needed both lists, for separate reasons. My cat's Bucket List contained the things I wanted him to be able to do before he passed, like stalk squirrels in the backyard. But when I wrote his Joy of Living list, I thought of the things that bring him joy all the time: sleeping on my laptop, basking in the sun on the picnic table, visits from my sister, and his favorite feather toy.

My cat's Joy of Living list helped me better assess his quality of life as his illness took its toll—were the things that brought him joy still bringing him joy? And when most of them didn't, that helped me better realize when it was time to say goodbye. I now encourage pet parents to create a Bucket List and a Joy of Living List (or Favorite Things!).

Cat Joys
of Living

 My cat Bodhi warming up on my laptop – one of his favorite things to do while I tried to work!"

.... 's
FAVORITE THINGS

PHOTO

- [ ]
- [ ]
- [ ]
- [ ]
- [ ]
- [ ]
- [ ]
- [ ]
- [ ]
- [ ]
- [ ]
- [ ]
- [ ]

13

Assessing your cat's life quality

The most common question pet parents ask me is "How will I know when it's time to say goodbye?" This is not an easy question to answer, and during my conversation with pet parents, we discuss life quality considerations in four major categories: the pet's ailments and the expected progression of each ailment, the pet's personality, the pet parent's personal beliefs about when to say goodbye, and the pet parent's ability to care for their pet in terms of their own essential pet care budgets—financial, time, physical, and emotional. How a pet parent wishes to say goodbye—euthanasia or natural passing—is another consideration. A helpful way to evaluate your cat's life quality is with one of the many assessment tools available from a variety of sources. I've created one here. You may want to use one or more different assessment methods to consider your cat's physical, mental, and emotional well-being.

Cat Life
Quality Tool

Cat Life Quality Assessment

Write "1"' in the appropriate column to the right of the assessment parameter. At the bottom you'll tally the columns and calculate your cat's score.

Category	My Cat...	Often	Sometimes	No/Not Applicable
SLEEPING	Wakes once or more at night and seems restless or anxious (paces, meows)			
	Sleeps more than usual during the day			
	Sleeps less than usual during the night			
MENTATION, ANXIETY, AND ACTIVITY	Wanders aimlessly around the house			
	Paces habitually in one location			
	Stares vacantly into space			
	Gets stuck or stands in corners or under furniture			
	Seems anxious, restless or unsettled during waking hours			
	Is more clingy than normal/seeks more attention			
	Shows less interest in exciting activities (greeting visitors, watching out the window, exploring new cardboard boxes or paper bags)			
	Seeks less attention than normal (love and pets)			
	Shows less interest in playing with toys			
	Meows for no apparent reason			
APPETITE AND THIRST	Has less interest in food or eats less than normal			
	Needs food to be warmed, or needs meat broth added to the food, or requires an appetite stimulant drug in order to eat			
	Needs to be hand-fed			
	Refuses to eat			
	Seems nauseous or vomits one or more times a week			
	Drinks water more often			
	Requires subcutaneous fluid therapy			

Category	My Cat...	Often	Sometimes	No/Not Applicable
ELIMINATION	Has diarrhea, or stool is soft and unformed			
	Has fecal incontinence one or more times a week			
	Urinates more than usual			
	Has urinary incontinence (dribbles urine after urinating normally or leaks urine while sleeping or resting)			
MOBILITY	Has difficulty lying down			
	Has difficulty getting up			
	Has difficulty walking up or down stairs			
	Drags toes when walking			
	Appears wobbly when walking			
	Cannot run and play like before			
	Cannot jump up to or down from favorite spots like before			
	Rarely or no longer uses a scratching post			
APPEARANCE	Looks thinner or less muscular			
	Has a dull facial expression, is not bright and alert			
	Hangs head and seems listless			
	Has a bad odor from skin, ears, or mouth			
	Appears unkempt, has a rough, matted or thin haircoat or hair loss			
	Has pressure sores or scabs			
BREATHING	Pants or open-mouth breathes			
	Tires easily with normal activity			
	Shows signs of difficulty breathing (anxious, wide-eyed expression, increased chest expansion and abdominal push when inhaling, abnormal gum or tongue color)			
	Sounds different when meowing (raspy, harsh, or squeaky)			
	Requires oxygen support			

Category	My Cat...	Often	Sometimes	No/Not Applicable
VISION	Has decreased vision			
	Bumps into objects, has difficulty finding bowls			
HEARING	Has decreased hearing			
	Startles easily when touched or seems less aware of approaching family members or other pets in the household			
PAIN OR DISCOMFORT	Is irritable or aggressive (growls, hisses, or bites at familiar people or pets)			
	Resists being petted			
	Resists being picked up			
	Sits in a hunched position with head lowered most of the time			
	Wants to be left alone or seeks hiding spots			

Total Assessment Factors	
Enter the total from the 'Often' column	
Halve the total from the Sometimes column. For example, if you answered "Sometimes'" 7 times, then enter 3.5.	
Add the value from the 'Often' column and the one-half value from the 'Sometimes' column. This is the total negative life quality score.	

Score interpretation	# of 'Negative Points'
Consider seeing your veterinarian to discuss the life quality factors you've marked.	Up to 8 points
Life quality is a concern, and your veterinarian can provide guidance on how to treat or help manage your cat's symptoms.	9–18 points
Life quality is deteriorating, and your cat would benefit from veterinary medical intervention to provide palliative care.	19–26 points
Life quality is poor. Consider veterinary hospice care or end-of-life discussions for your cat with your veterinarian.	27–36 points
Life quality is extremely poor. Consider euthanasia or palliative supported natural passing.	More than 36 points

14

Caring for caregivers

Throughout my career, I've helped countless families navigate the complexities of caring for their chronically ailing or terminally ill pets. I've seen how caregiving can strain a pet parent's emotions, physical ability, finances, and work and leisure schedules. Caring for an ailing cat is not easy. It can tax your relationships with family members, friends, and your cat. Managing a cat's intense needs can be rewarding, but it can also negatively impact your quality of life.

I've also taken on the role of intense caregiver for many of my own pets. I've mostly experienced enthusiasm, pride, joy, and contentment as their caregiver. And even though I love to do it, it's still a hard job. At times I've also been a tired, frustrated, mad, and stressed caregiver for my pets.

The number one reason why pet parents elect euthanasia for their cat is their cat's decreased quality of life. The number two reason is caregiver burden. If you're unable to take care of yourself, you'll be unable to care for others. I've created a chart to help you identify and reflect on some of the challenges and stressful feelings you may experience as you care for your ailing cat. My intention is not to determine whether you've had enough or whether you can handle more, because that is your personal decision. My intention is to help you remember you aren't alone in having these feelings.

Cat Caregiver
QOL

My hope is that in recognizing these challenges and feelings, you'll share them with your family, friends, and veterinary team to identify whether and what types of additional support may be available.

50

Caregiver Assessment Chart

Category	I...	Often	Sometimes	No, or not applicable to me or my family
SLEEPING	Wake up one or more times a night to help my cat into the litter box or clean up an accident			
	Wake up one or more times a night to comfort my cat			
THOUGHTS	Worry about my cat when I am not home			
	Have to frequently monitor my cat's activities or whereabouts			
	Find my cat's confusion or disorientation difficult to manage			
	Am worried my cat is suffering			
	Am unsure how to evaluate my cat's happiness			
	Am irritated by my cat's loud howling			
MANAGING MY CAT'S APPETITE, THIRST, MEDICATIONS, OTHER THERAPY	Have a hard time getting my cat to eat			
	Spend extra time preparing my cat's food			
	Am worried my cat is not eating enough			
	Am worried my cat is not drinking enough water			
	Struggle to give my cat medications			
	Have a hard time giving my cat subcutaneous fluids			
	Have a hard time giving my cat oxygen therapy			
	Have a hard time giving my cat physical therapy or massage			
MANAGING MY CAT'S CLEANLINESS AND APPEARANCE	Often have to clean up my cat's urine or fecal accidents			
	Have a hard time keeping my cat clean			
	Often have to clean up my cat's vomit			
	Have to restrict my cat to a certain area or limit access in my home			
	Have a hard time keeping my cat's resting or sleeping areas clean			
	Am worried that my cat looks sick			
	Have a hard time brushing my cat			
	Cannot handle the way my cat smells			
	Am embarrassed to have visitors because of my cat's appearance, odor, or behavior			

Category	I...	Often	Sometimes	No, or not applicable to me or my family
MOBILITY	Have a hard time helping my cat get up on favorite spots			
	Have a hard time helping my cat use stairs			
	Am unable to play with my cat because of my cat's physical limitations			
HOUSEHOLD	Hear from others in my household who are angry with the cat			
	Have arguments about my cat's care with family or friends			
	Have to hide or quickly clean up my cat's accidents so others don't see them			
	Have to warn or protect other pets, family members or friends because my cat may bite or scratch them			
	Have a hard time making physical adjustments in the household to meet my cat's mobility or comfort needs			
	Have a hard time making schedule adjustments in the household to meet my cat's needs			
THOUGHTS ABOUT CARING FOR MY CAT OVERALL	Am stressed by the amount of care my cat needs			
	Feel overwhelmed by the amount of care my cat needs			
	No longer wish to be my cat's caregiver			
	Would like or need more emotional support from others in providing care for my cat			
	Would like or need more physical help from others in providing care for my cat			
	Am struggling with anticipatory grief (feel overly anxious or depressed about the time I have left with my cat)			
	Feel anger toward my cat			
	Feel guilt about my cat's condition			
	Am worried I will allow my cat to suffer			
	Need help determining when it is time to say goodbye to my cat			

Category	I...	Often	Sometimes	No, or not applicable to me or my family
BUDGETS	Cannot financially care properly for my cat			
	Cannot physically care properly for my cat			
	Cannot take the amount of time needed to properly care for my cat			
	Cannot emotionally care properly for my cat			

Total Assessment Factors	
Enter the total from the 'Often" column	
Halve the total from the Sometimes column. For example, if you answered "Sometimes'" 7 times, then enter 3.5.	
Add the value from the 'Often' column and the one-half value from the 'Sometimes' column. This is the total negative life quality score.	

The strain of caring for your pet is highly subjective. What one person can handle and what another can manage can be completely different. There is no 'wrong' way to feel. I believe it is good to ask yourself all of the questions above to honestly assess the different stressors you are dealing with—and maybe seek help with caregiving to help lighten the burden.

Below was my personal scoring system when managing my own cat's terminal illness. It may be helpful to you.

Caregiver Assessment	# of 'Negative Points'
You're managing your cat's ailments well. Consider talking with your veterinarian for additional suggestions that may make your cat's ailments easier to manage.	up to 10 points
The strain of caring for your cat may be negatively affecting your life quality. Make sure your cat is receiving medical attention so that ailments are managed appropriately. Look into ways to get help and take care of yourself.	11 - 20 points
Caring for your cat is negatively affecting your life quality. Remember, it's OK to be frustrated, sad, angry, confused, and a myriad of other emotions. It's also OK to consider end-of-life decisions for your cat, because their life quality is probably also quite diminished.	21 - 30 points
Consider euthanasia or palliative supported natural passing for your cat.	over 30 points

15

Cat days

Pet parents commonly tell me, "When my cat has more bad days than good days, then I will know it's time to say goodbye." In this case, it's important to measure what you're monitoring, because it can be difficult to accurately determine, "Is my cat having more bad days than good days?"

Using a simple tracking system such as a calendar helps. First write down what makes up a good day for your cat and you. This is different for everyone and every cat. Do you need your cat to sleep through the night to call it a good day, or are you happy with four hours of sleep? Does a good day mean no accidents outside the litter box, or is an occasional mess OK? Is it a good day when your cat eats every meal, or a bad day if he refuses even one? Everyone in your household should agree on the definition of a good day. Then begin marking the bad days on a calendar. You can then divide the number of good days by the number of bad days to determine your cat's quality of life score as listed on the next page. I suggest placing the calendar (you can copy or print out the template I provide here) somewhere easily visible, such as on your refrigerator. Simply write an 'X' or a sad face on a bad day, or write brief notes that describe the good and bad about the day.

Cat Calendar

You can also look into the app Grey Muzzle which allows you to make a profile for your cat and keep a daily calendar on your phone: www.drmarygardner.com/greymuzzle

QUALITY OF LIFE CALENDAR

MONTH

M	T	W	T	F	S	S

YOUR PET'S QUALITY
OF LIFE SCORE $= \dfrac{\text{GOOD DAYS}}{\text{BAD DAYS}}$

NOTES

>2	Good quality of life
1.1-2	More good days than bad days but monitor quality of life
1	Good days = bad days
.5-.9	Bad days outnumber good days
.1-.4	Quality of life is not well. Discuss with a veterinarian.
0	No good days at all. Palliative sedation or euthanasia are warranted.

Dr Mary   www.drmarygardner.com

About Dr. Mary Gardner

Dr. Mary Gardner graduated from the University of Florida College of Veterinary Medicine and began her veterinary career in a small animal primary care practice in South Florida. She then turned her professional focus to pet hospice and palliative care. Known to her patients' families as Dr. Mary, she is cofounder of Lap of Love Veterinary Hospice, the nation's largest organization of veterinarians dedicated to in-home end-of-life veterinary care for pets. Lap of Love also provides teleadvice and pet loss support services.

Dr. Mary and Lap of Love have been featured in *Entrepreneur Magazine*, *The New York Times*, and numerous professional veterinary publications, and on the show *The Doctors*. Dr. Mary has written hundreds of articles for veterinary publications and is a coauthor and editor of a textbook for veterinarians, *Treatment and Care of the Veterinary Geriatric Patient*. She is author of two books for pet parents of elderly dogs, *It's Never Long Enough: A Practical Guide to Caring for Your Geriatric Dog*, and *Geriatric Dog Health & Care Journal: A Complete Toolkit for the Geriatric Dog Caregiver*. Dr. Mary is also coauthor of an activity book that supports a child's journey through grief after saying goodbye to a beloved dog, *Forever Friend*.

Dr. Mary has taught at hundreds of veterinary medical conferences, veterinary schools, and pet events to share her knowledge on enhancing care for aging pets, caring for caregivers, and easing the final goodbye. She was named Small Animal Speaker of the Year in 2020 at VMX, one of the largest veterinary conferences in the world.

Dr. Mary has helped elevate the attention, medical care, and support that veterinarians and pet owners provide for senior pets. She shares her Florida home with cats who can be found lounging in her bed, on her laptop, in a sunbeam, or snuggled up with one of her dogs. You can follow her (@drmarygardner) on Instagram, Facebook and YouTube. Check out her website www.drmarygardner.com or her Pinterest page @greymuzzlevet.

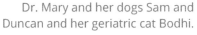 Dr. Mary and her dogs Sam and Duncan and her geriatric cat Bodhi.

Made in United States
Orlando, FL
03 October 2022